DAMN YOU, AUTOCORRECT!

Momma

Are u sore

Do ducks have jackets

Did muck save maggots

Ughhhh

Does husk make gaggles

Never mind

what

what...I just..what.

DAMN YOU, AUTOCORRECT!

Awesomely Embarrassing Text Messages
You Didn't Mean to Send

Jillian
Madison

hachette
BOOKS

NEW YORK BOSTON

Hachette Books
Hachette Book Group
1290 Avenue of the Americas
New York, NY 10104
www.HachetteBookGroup.com

Printed in the United States of America

RRD-C

Originally published by Hyperion.
First Hachette Books edition: February 2015

20   19   18   17   16   15   14   13   12

Hachette Books is a division of Hachette Book Group, Inc.
The Hachette Books name and logo are trademarks of Hachette Book Group, Inc.

The publisher is not responsible for websites (or their content) that are not owned by the publisher.

Madison, Jillian.
    Damn you, autocorrect! : awesomely embarrassing text messages you didn't mean to send / Jillian Madison. — 1st ed.
        p. cm.
ISBN 978-1-4013-1067-7
    1. Text messages (Telephone systems) — Humor.   I. Title.
    PN6231.T565M34 2011
    818'.60208—dc22

                                        2011014361

Design by Sunil Manchikanti

Dedications

To Mom & Dad.
Thank you for not owning smartphones, and for
only mildly freaking out when I shunned corporate
life to "work on the internets."

To Michelle.
Get ready, because tonight, we're goin' TOMCAT.

To Brie.
My best friend, and the most amazing
woodchuck you will ever meet.
I meant woman! Damn you, Autocorrect!

And to everyone who contributed to the website and this book.
Thank you for not proofreading before hitting send.
Text on, motherduckers!

Contents

Introduction

"DAMN YOU, AUTOCORRECT!"

If you own a smartphone, there's a good chance you've screamed that phrase at least once. Maybe you sent a text to your spouse that you "f'd the dog" (fed) or fired off a note to a co-worker about your "bad case of the manboobs" (Mondays). Either way, Autocorrect was likely the culprit.

While the feature on our mobile devices can be a blessing, it's also often a curse. It frequently changes words without rhyme or reason, and if you hit "send" too quickly, it can lead to some funny, confusing, or just plain embarrassing results. I found that out the hard way in the summer of 2010 when I innocently tried to invite a few friends over for an evening of gelato. My iPhone's Autocorrect, however, had another idea and asked them over for a night of "fellatio." And just like that, Autocorrect turned me into a hussy. What would my mother say!

Shortly after the gelato/fellatio incident, I started wondering if other people out there were having similar experiences with their smartphones. So I purchased the www.damnyouautocorrect.com domain, set up the site on a whim, and added about fifteen Autocorrect incidents involving myself and my friends. I could never have anticipated the public's reaction. As it turned out, there were millions of people who were just as frustrated by Autocorrect as I was.

By the end of its first week online, DamnYouAutoCorrect .com earned write-ups on ABC, CNN, Gizmodo, Mashable, *The Huffington Post*, and in dozens of other national media outlets. It went viral on Twitter and Facebook and, literally overnight, found itself getting over 1 million page views and five hundred submissions per day from people all over the globe. Those numbers have been steadily increasing every week.

I think DamnYouAutocorrect.com immediately struck a chord because people of every age can relate to it. These days, everyone texts, and the content highlights situations we've all been in ourselves. And even if we haven't, it's just human nature to enjoy voyeuristically peering in on the hilarious—and often cringe-worthy—text fails our peers have experienced.

And there have been some real doozies. This book is packed with three hundred hilarious images—most of which are found for the first time here—that highlight the unintentional hilarity that often ensues when Autocorrect goes wrong. These laugh-out-loud funny examples include:

- Co-workers talking about their "ejaculation" reports (escalation);
- A husband texting his wife that he "laid" the baby-sitter (paid);
- A cook warning someone not to touch a bowl of "masturbating" cherries (macerating);
- And of course, friends complaining about how much they hate the dreaded "auto erection" feature on their smartphone.

And then there's the most popular image on the DamnYouAutoCorrect.com website to date: a father texting his daughter that he and his mother were going to divorce, when they were in fact just going to *Disney*. Oops! I'll take "texts I wouldn't want to receive" for $200 please, Alex.

BUT WHAT IS AUTOCORRECT, ANYWAY?

Autocorrect is a software function—commonly found on many smartphones and portable web-ready devices like the iPod Touch—that attempts to correct common typos on the fly by guessing the word you were really trying to write. In theory, Autocorrect's ultimate goal is to save time by automating spell check functions and offering predictions, often before you've even finished typing the entire word. But is this feature really improving our modern, super-connected lives?

We move fast, talk fast, and type fast, and there's no denying Autocorrect can be a huge help in certain circumstances. It often works as the silent hero in the background, making otherwise illegible sentences like "Ehag timr is yge mewtigg" show up properly as: "What time is the meeting?"

But not so fast! Unlike Jennifer Aniston's hair, Autocorrect isn't always perfect. It has a sinister side too—one that steps in and inserts completely inappropriate words that can make you look like an idiot, a creep, or (gasp!) a total pervert. The iPhone, for example, frequently autocorrects "Whitehouse" to "whorehouse" and "homie" to "homoerotic." If you hit "send" without carefully proofreading, the conversation will certainly take an interesting turn. And so might your evening.

OKAY, SO HOW DOES AUTOCORRECT WORK?

As it stands right now, it's almost impossible to find information about exactly how the elusive Autocorrect feature works. It's a closely guarded trade secret among the mobile phone companies and software developers, and most of them are incredibly tight-lipped when it comes to discussing it.

What we do know is that when you start typing a word, the Autocorrect software checks those letters against a built-in dictionary. If it doesn't find an exact match, it guesses what you were trying to type and offers that word up as a suggestion. Many smart phones also have some sort of "learning" element as well, meaning they add new words and terms to the dictionary based on the user's behaviors and patterns of use. As a result, after a period of acclimation, no two Autocorrect dictionaries may ever be alike. That means if you're frequently using words like "anal" or "vagina," there may be an increased risk of your Autocorrect, uh, slipping those words in during future conversations. Sexters, beware!

HOW CAN THINGS GO SO WRONG?

Autocorrect seemingly has a mind of its own—and as you'll see in this book, often a hilariously *dirty* one. The real trouble comes when you hit "send" without realizing the word you thought you typed was swapped out for something else. For me, there are two fundamental problems with the way the feature works on the device:

First, when you're typing, you're instinctively looking down at the keypad. The autocorrected suggestions, however, show up in the message area, making them incredibly easy to miss if you're typing quickly and not paying close attention. Second, when typing, all you have to do to accept the word suggestion is tap the space bar. That's it! The only way to get rid of the Autocorrect suggestion is to keep typing more letters, or to hit the little "x" next to the suggested word in the bubble. That's just not intuitive at all. Often, you think you're ignoring the word suggestion by just hitting "space" and continuing to type your message. But you've done just the opposite. The rest, as they say, is history. You've just been "Autocorrected," my friend!

HOLY MOLYBDENUM! THAT'S TOTALLY HOOSEGOW!

DamnYouAutoCorrect.com receives about six hundred new submissions per day from the website and the iPhone/iPod Touch app, and I read every one of them myself to determine if they're website-worthy (hey, it's a hilarious job, but somebody's gotta do it). I've noticed several trends by doing all that reading, one of which is the relatively new "extra letters" phenomenon, in which the more you repeat the letter, the more strongly you mean it. For example, people frequently write the phrase: "let's gooooooooooooo!" Autocorrect dictionaries have no clue how to handle all those extra letters, and on the iPhone, it's often autocorrected to "let's hookup" or "let's hippopotamus"—either one of which might be incredibly embarrassing, especially if you're talking to a relative or a zookeeper. But that's a topic for another book.

Smartphones also love to insert nonsensical, totally random words that have absolutely nothing to do with what you're talking about. Did someone say something funny? Be careful when replying back with "hahahaha," because it's often autocorrected to "Shabaka"—an Egyptian pharaoh back in 700 BC. The word "hilarious" often gets autocorrected to "hoosegow"—a slang term for a prison. And for all my science geeks in the house (holler!), try typing "holy moly" into your phone. On my device, I end up with "holy molybdenum," the chemical element with the atomic number 42. But I'm sure you already knew that.

Science not your thing? Are you more of a sports buff? Just make sure you double-check your messages before you hit "send" on your iPhone, or you might find yourself talking about Derek Heterosexual (Jeter), Juan Urine (Uribe), or the great play you just saw the Boners (Niners) complete. Take my word for it—your friends will never let you live it down.

Many devices really seem to struggle with pop culture references too. For example, I use Twitter all the time, and no matter how many times I hit that little "x" to dismiss the suggested word, my iPhone tries to change the word "tweeting" (the process of sending Twitter messages) to "teething" and the word "retweet" to "retarded." Try explaining *that* one to your unsuspecting friends and followers.

Based on my observations with Autocorrect and the submissions sent into DamnYouAutoCorrect.com, these are the top twenty-five most common Autocorrect mishaps:

Word / phrase you're trying to write	Autocorrected to
Hell	He'll
A sec	Asexual or a sex
Awwwww	Sewers
Thing	Thong
Bitch	Birch
Give me a call	Give me anal
Oooohhh	Pooping
Grrr	Ferret
Whenever	Wieners
Pick me up	Oil me up
Keys	Jews
Shit	Shot
Coworkers	Visigoths or Coriander
Goooooo	Hookup
Fucking	Ducking
Hahahaha	Shabaka
Homie	Homoerotic
Sodium	Sodomy
Mani/Pedi	Mani/Penis
Pen	Penis
Yesyes	Testes
Soonish	Zionism
Netflix	Negroid
Kids	LSD
Parents	Parrots

Another thing that drives people "ducking" nuts about the iPhone—and a trend you may have noticed in the above list—is its almost comical aversion to swearing. It hates curse words, and does everything in its "ducking" power to prevent you from using them. It even goes so far as to insert an apostrophe in the word HELL (HE'LL), which obviously makes the word take on an entirely different meaning. Its desire to keep things PG-13 is often infuriating, because let's face it: Sometimes you just need to call someone a fucking asshole.

So now that you know what Autocorrect is and how it works, you're ready to get to the submissions. Just remember: If you don't want to end up like one of the poor motherduckers in this book, type carefully and proofread your messages . . . or you too might one day find yourself screaming: "DAMN YOU, AUTO-CORRECT!"

Peace out, homoerotic! And if you don't like this book, you can go to he'll! Shabaka!

Parents Just Don't Understand:

Awkward Texts with Mom & Dad

Mom's Office Fight

Do Ducks Have Jackets?

PARENTS JUST DON'T UNDERSTAND

Way TMI for Dad

16

PARENTS JUST DON'T UNDERSTAND

Happy Birthday, Mom

DAMN YOU, AUTOCORRECT!

Messages from Beyond

Messages · **Mom** · **Edit**

Jun 21, 2010 9:07 PM

The grave is open

What grave?????

Oops garage

Ohhhh....... That makes more sense and isn't as creepy !

PARENTS JUST DON'T UNDERSTAND

Shopping for Dad

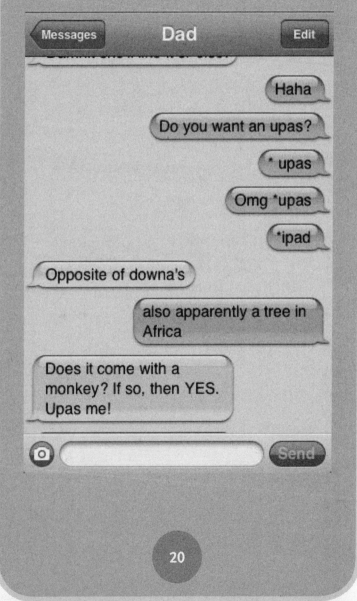

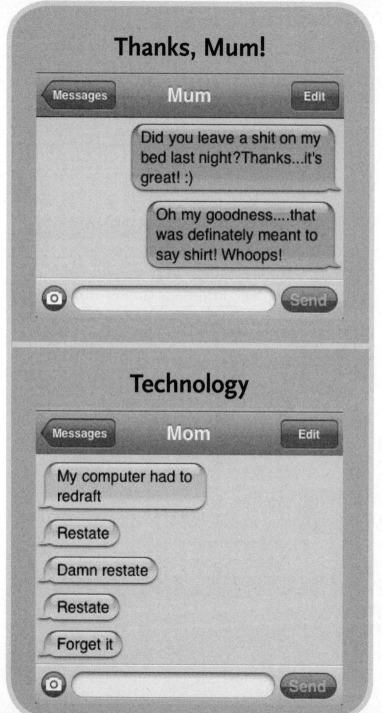

PARENTS JUST DON'T UNDERSTAND

Dinner Options

needs info about your school books.
Wed, Oct 13, 2010, 7:09 PM

Thu, Oct 14, 2010

 Mom: U desire which day it coming home? Was thinking of vagina chicken for dinner tonite...

.
Thu, Oct 14, 2010, 12:21 PM

 Me: Reread that text
Thu, Oct 14, 2010, 12:24 PM

Mom: Whoops...! Did u get a good laugh out of it?and did u understand what I meant?
Thu, Oct 14, 2010, 12:26 PM

 Me: Yes, and so did everyone else in the lobby. And I have no idea what you meant
Thu, Oct 14, 2010, 12:27 PM

Sat, Oct 16, 2010

DAMN YOU, AUTOCORRECT!

22

Accidental Insult

Chew on This

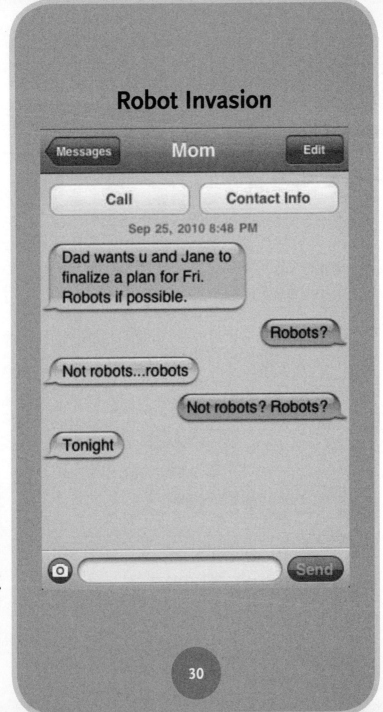

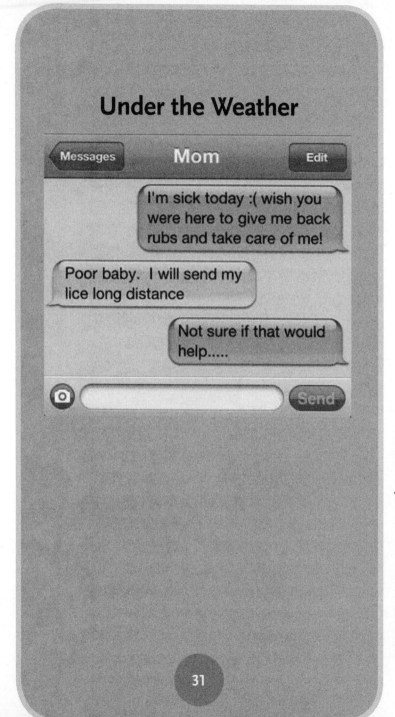

Under the Weather

PARENTS JUST DON'T UNDERSTAND

PARENTS JUST DON'T UNDERSTAND

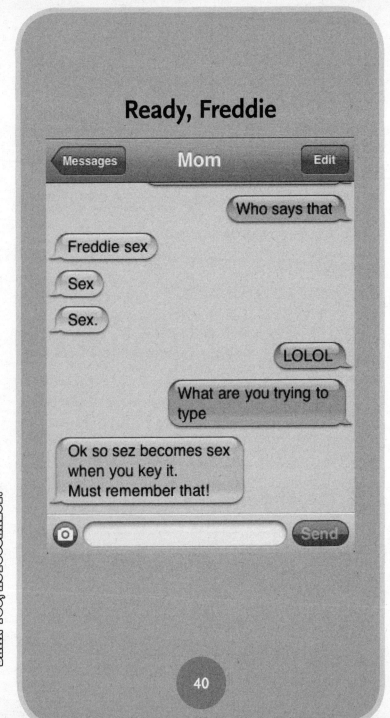

Dad's Wish List

PARENTS JUST DON'T UNDERSTAND

PARENTS JUST DON'T UNDERSTAND

When Dads Shop...

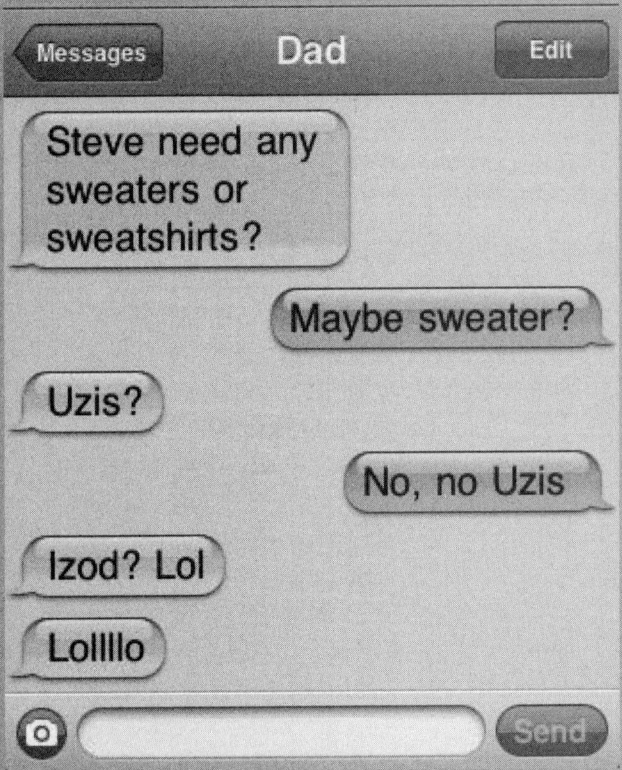

Messages   Dad   Edit

Steve need any sweaters or sweatshirts?

Maybe sweater?

Uzis?

No, no Uzis

Izod? Lol

Lollllo

DAMN YOU, AUTOCORRECT!

50

Fourth of July

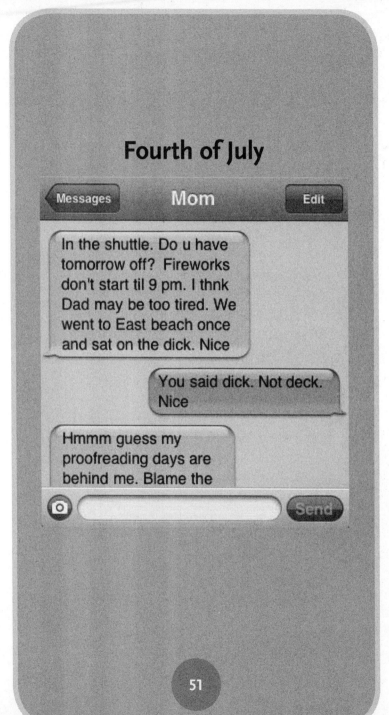

Mom

In the shuttle. Do u have tomorrow off? Fireworks don't start til 9 pm. I thnk Dad may be too tired. We went to East beach once and sat on the dick. Nice

You said dick. Not deck. Nice

Hmmm guess my proofreading days are behind me. Blame the

Send

PARENTS JUST DON'T UNDERSTAND

Congrats—Love Dad

PARENTS JUST DON'T UNDERSTAND

Christmas Presents

Love Gone Wrong:

When Couples Text

Autocorrect & Relationship Advice Don't Mix

Call   Contact Info

12 Nov 2010 15:15

Don't worry, seriously. He's crazy about you and he loves you so much. He told me the other day that you're the first girl he had ever thought about the führer with. Xx

WTF?

Ok so that was supposed to say future... Damn Phone! Xx

LOVE GONE WRONG

Arguing Over Text

Nov 11, 2010 4:30 PM

First I'm not going to do this over text messaging second stop being mad about it get over it. It's done.

I'm done texting I have a busy night and a slut to do. If you want to call me you can around 8-830

I love u

You have a slut to do? Wow now I'm really mad at you.

Delete   Forward

61

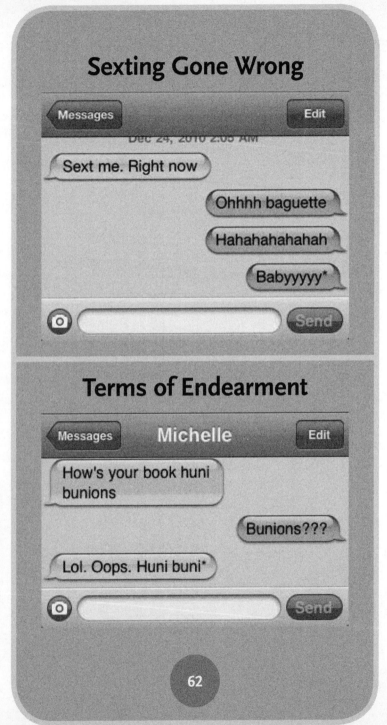

A Night Apart

Messages Jen Edit

I'm home safely! I hope you got your key situation worked out. love you!! miss you tons already :)

Yay I'm glad!! :) I miss you tooo! Cockfight

cock fight?

Hahahaha it was supposed to be xoxoxoxo

I like cock fight better.

Haha okay :) I'm seriously busting up laughing

Send

The Babysitter

Messages | John | Edit

Did you guys eat dinner yet?

Yep. Just had pasta.

Oh by the way, I laid the babysitter.

Uh, excuse me? You fucking what?????

Hahah PAID. I paid her. Sorry to give you a heart attack babe.

I hate you! lol

Send

Now THAT'S Love

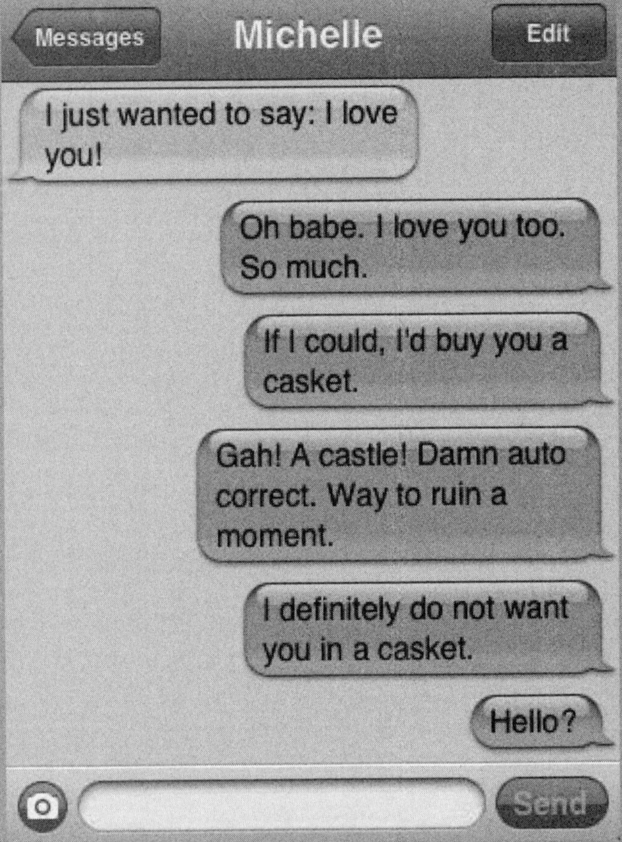

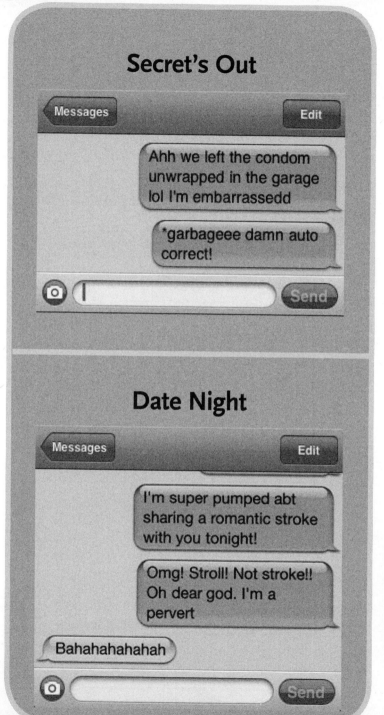

A Night In

Hidden Desires

Greg

> Hey! Around what time will you be here?

Mornin baby! I'm just leavin my place now so... About 15 mins.

> Ok! Are you hungry? Cuz i really want a baby!

A baby? Dear god please tell me that was auto correct

> Hahahahahah. I meant a bagel. Not a baby. Well maybe someday

The Crush

Drunk Dialing

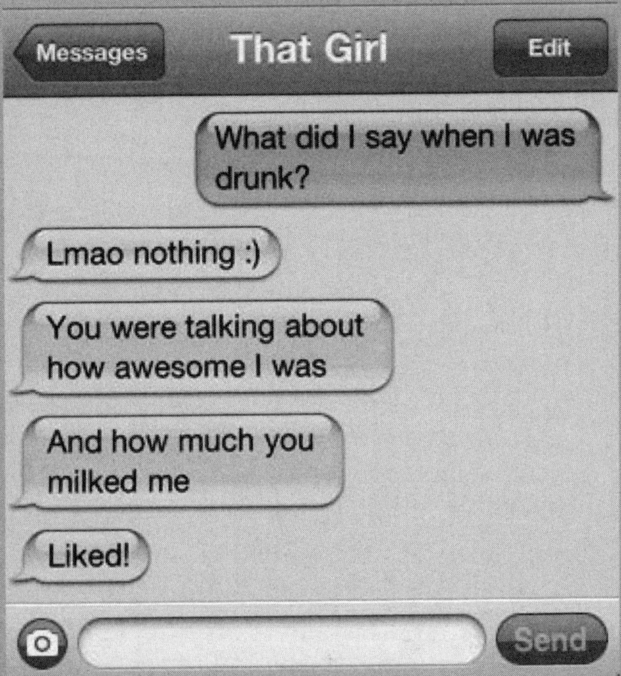

Messages
That Girl
Edit
What did I say when I was drunk?
Lmao nothing :)
You were talking about how awesome I was
And how much you milked me
Liked!
Send

The Mall & More

I need to go to the mall but my sis has the car. Can u take me babe?

Yea I wanna go buy a game anyway. I'll oil your ass up in 45 mins!

Lol I wrote pick you up. In 45.

Good bc there will be no oiling of my ass in 45 mins or ever! Xo

Bedtime Wishes

Grocery Shopping

Messages Edit

Be home soon. Do you want anything from whore foods?

If you're at whore foods I'll take something tall and blonde.

But if you're at whole foods I'll take some peanut butter.

Send

A New Measure of Time

Backhanded Compliment

LOVE GONE WRONG

Bad Kissers

LOVE GONE WRONG

LOVE GONE WRONG

So Romantic

3

What's Cookin':

Autocorrected Food & Beverage Texts

Don't Touch the Bowl!

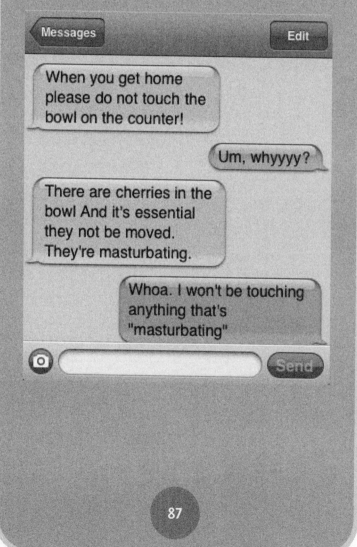

WHAT'S COOKIN'

Anniversary Meal

WHAT'S COOKIN'

Bomb Squad

Messages
Matthew
Edit
Can you please take out the hamburger to thaw out. I'm going to make spaghetti tonight.
Dec 14, 2010 12:22 PM
Did you set out hamburger for tonight?
Dec 14, 2010 1:44 PM
Hello?? You there??
Dec 14, 2010 2:31 PM
Hamburger is detonated
Dec 14, 2010 3:09 PM
What??
Lol not frozen
Send

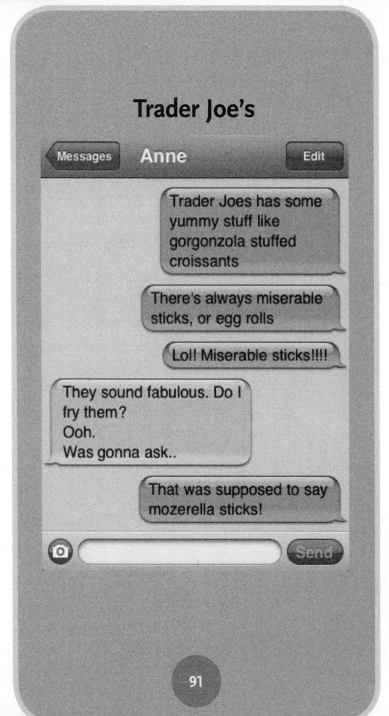

WHAT'S COOKIN'

Rosemary and Rhyme

Romantic Dinner

WHAT'S COOKIN'

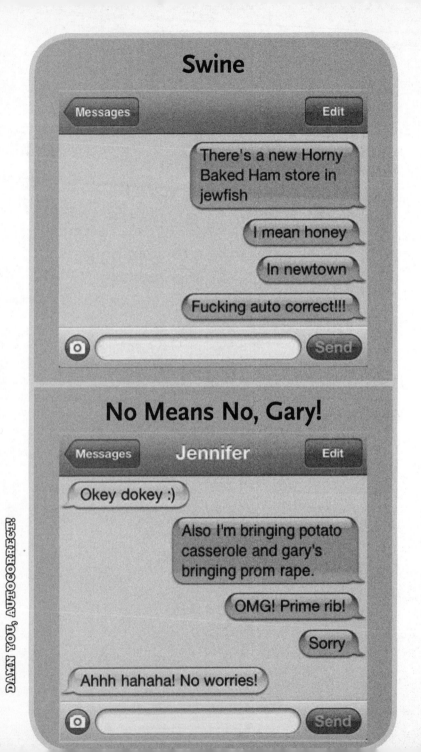

Odd Donut Shop Order

WHAT'S COOKIN'

Empty Fridge

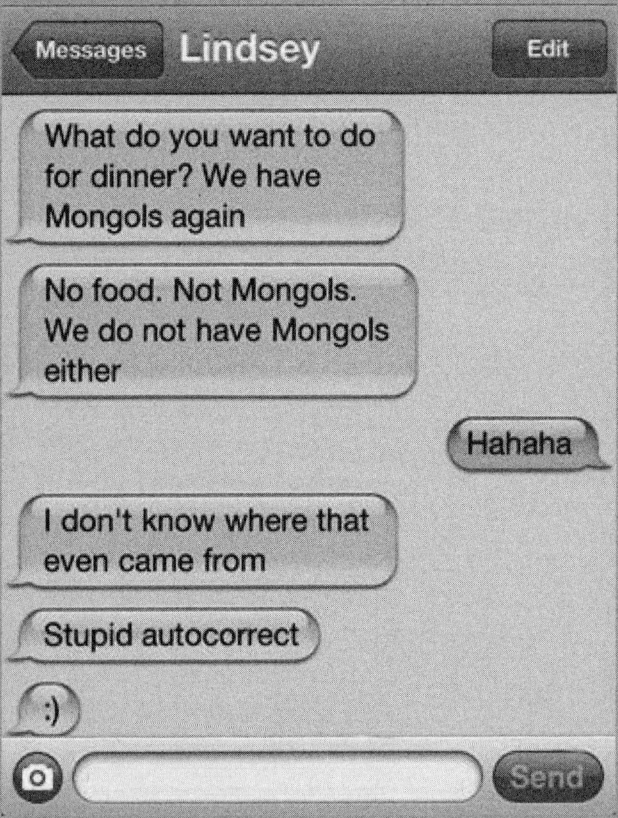

Messages
Lindsey
Edit
What do you want to do for dinner? We have Mongols again
No food. Not Mongols. We do not have Mongols either
Hahaha
I don't know where that even came from
Stupid autocorrect
:)
Send

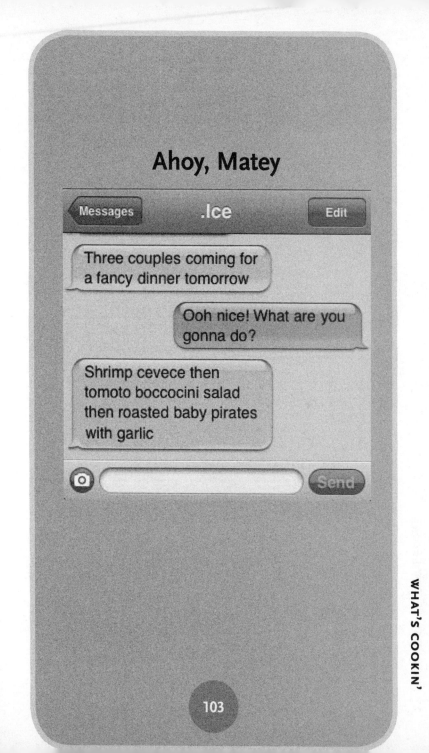

WHAT'S COOKIN'

Shopping List

Dec 31, 2010 1:54 PM

Ok, also need canola oil, another pack of wonton wrappers, pepperoni, onion, unwanted butter and a small thing of shortening (I think they make a little crisco can.

No butter is ever unwanted

Unsalted maybe... Unwanted - never!

That cracks me up! Unwanted.

Goddammit! UnSALTED.

Snack Time

What are you brining to the party? I'm making camel balls now. Cant wait for you to try them! They are to die for!

I donno about camel balls. Eeek!

HAAAAA! I meant "caramel bars" not balls! I wouldn't even know where to get the ingredients for "camel balls".

DAMN YOU, AUTOCORRECT!

108

Mom's Hungry

How to Cook Lentils

I've cooked the soup for over the time it said & the lentils are still hard ... : (
Do you know anything about cooking lentils

hmmm...you might not have pee-soaked them, so it'll take longer to cook. make sure they're rotating in the broth, otherwise it's not hot enough. just takes a while babe : /

pre-soaked!!!! gahhhh! smart type sucks!!!

No Soup for You

WHAT'S COOKIN'

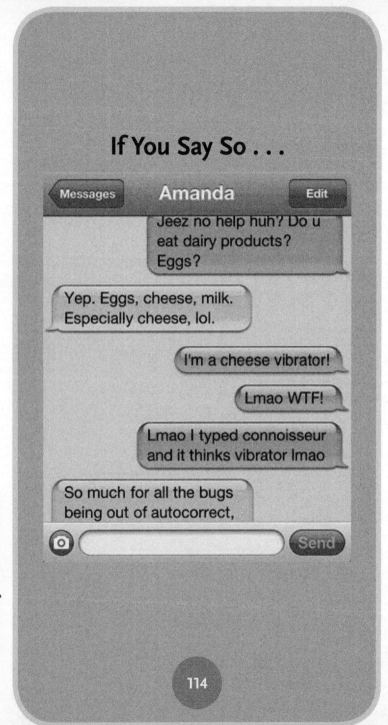

New Side Dish Sweeping the Nation

They are having roast beef, mashed fatties, green beans, rolls, etc. Do you want me to bring some home or you want something else?

Sounds good.

But what are mashed fatties?

I meant tatties.

Taters? Lol!

Or Taters.

Send

DAMN YOU, AUTOCORRECT!

4

**Freudian
Slips:**

When Autocorrect
Reads Your Mind

Boob Tube

Game Night

To: Kingsdaddy > Deborah > Hide
Jtown > Pattypoo > Picky >
Mikeyboo > Charlie Bones > Jroo >
Bekah > Jooooosh >

Hey all. Bisexuals night tomorrow night at 830 who's in? Lemme know. Or don't let me know. Your choice.

Ok well that's weird. Ummm that was supposed to say boardgame not bisexuals soooo BOARDGAME

Send

DAMN YOU, AUTOCORRECT!

124

FREUDIAN SLIPS

Such a Hassle

Dirty Mind

Planning the Evening

Messages **Chris** Edit

Dec 28, 2010 12:52 PM

Hi! Answer.

Haha, what time did you want to leave for the bar on nye? I know Brian has to work until 6, and I'm trying to figure out what time everyone else will be down so we have enough time to orgasm

AH!!!! Damn autocorrect! Pregame*** pregame!!!

HAHAHAHAHAHAHAHA.

Send

FREUDIAN SLIPS

Working Up a Thirst

FREUDIAN SLIPS

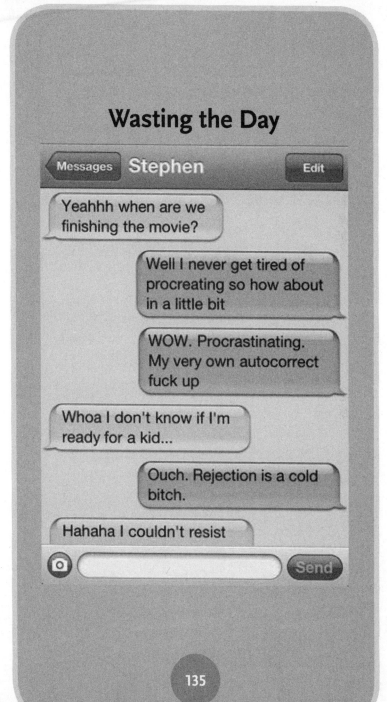

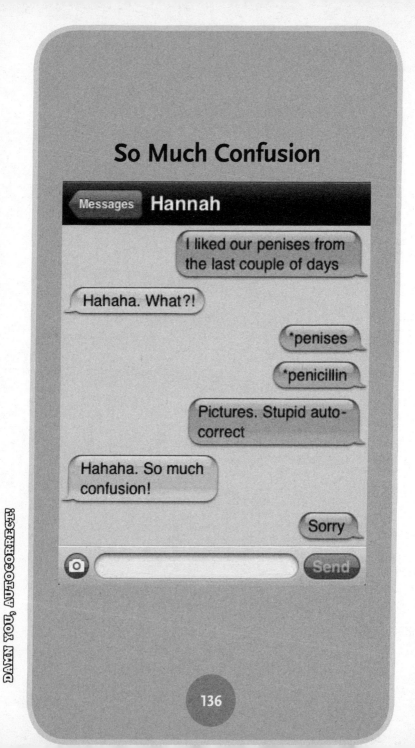

FREUDIAN SLIPS

FREUDIAN SLIPS

Crash and Burn

Beware of Santa

Hahahhahaha damn I coulda looked for Santa longer!

I am about to go out. I will look for him!

Hahaha he might attempt to rub you over.

I mean run.

If Santa rubs me... I better get everything I want for Christmas.

I need to stop using my phone. I fail at doing so correctly.

FREUDIAN SLIPS

Two Hours

Heyyyyyy

What's up? I was just gonna call you.

Nothin! Bored. Mikes been in here making me orgasm for the past two hours.

What!?

OMGOMG I meant origami. From the book I got him for Xmas! LMFAo

Two hours? Wow impressive. If he has a brother tell him to call me.

Welcome to the Neighborhood

FREUDIAN SLIPS

The Holidays

Remedy for a Sore Throat

Interesting Turn of Events

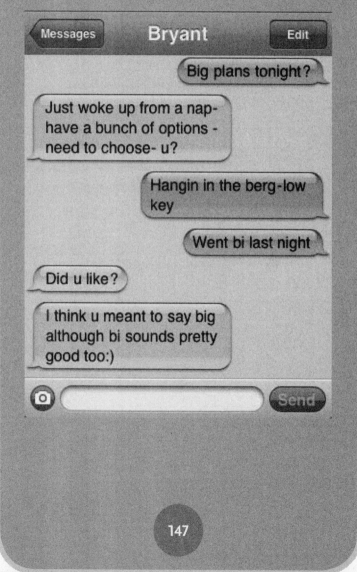

Open Schedule

FREUDIAN SLIPS

Can You Sense It?

So sure

Hahaha. I hope you can sense the orgasm through the texts.

Oh. My. God! I totally meant sarcasm!!!!! Stupid Phone spell check! I don't even know how that popped up.

Haha oh yeah

Bahaha. That was embarrassiiiiiiiing.

Send

DAMN YOU, AUTOCORRECT!

Thanks for Sharing

Take Your Time

Messages · Cristina · Edit

Text me before you head over. Gotta rub out for a sec

Omg I man RUN out.. Hahaha

Mean

Hahaha!! I'll give u all the time u need ;) wow.

Send

Reminders

5 Dec 2010 11:55 PM

Remind me to find a penis for English timorousness

Penis not penis and tomorrow****

FFS! penis***

Penis*********

Ahh fuck this pics of ship crapple phone :@

Ffs!!!!! Shit*** piece****

Subject

Send

153

FREUDIAN SLIPS

Dangers of Kickboxing

John wants me to take this kickboxing class with him.

I don't really want to but he's pushing me.

You totally should. It's fun and a great workout. Why don't you want to

I know but I don't wanna get him in my mouth

What sorta class is that?!

Omg *hit!!! In my mouth.

Send

5

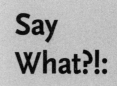

Say
What?!:

Totally Random
Autocorrect Incidents

Shabaka!

SAY WHAT?!

Dancing Queen

Let's Talk About Plants, Baby

Sounds Serious

SAY WHAT?!

Zionism

Fuzzy Flowers

this is gonna be all you hear about in nerdland when the USA version drops. The books, of course, are already HUGE beardtongues.

what in the fuck?

HOW IN THE SHIT DID "BESTSELLERS" GET AUTOCORRECTED TO "BEARDTONGUES"?

I do not know and am horrified.

Send

DAMN YOU, AUTOCORRECT!

BADONKADONK!

Don't Be a Joe Bagel

goddess Hahahahahaha

Hahaha yay I feel like a classy lady haha

Hahahahahaha classy ladies can be sexy too. Jesus I can't win with you. I didn't say hoe bag lol

No I was being serious! I know I'm not a Joe bagel

Fuck! Joe bag

Nipple tots! Hoe bag

Tits!!! Forget this phone

Hahahaha nipple tots?

Send

Pizza Toppings

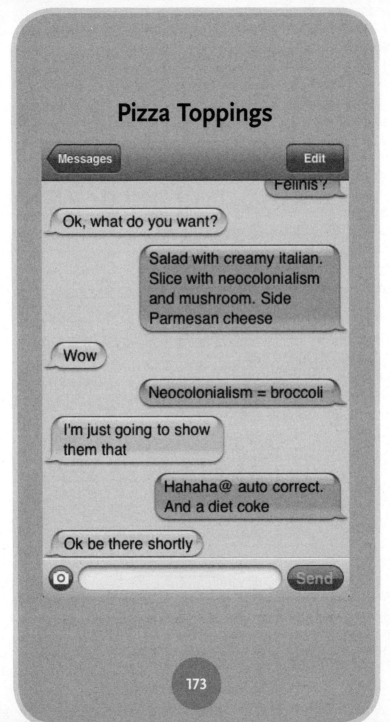

SAY WHAT?!

Yellow Flowering Plants

DAMN YOU, AUTOCORRECT!

Baby, It's Cold Outside

Omg, heated mattress pad. My life will never be the same. Such magic.

Thank you thankkkkkk you

Nov 30, 2010 10:13 AM

Obama guessing that you were not cold last night?

*I'm a - not Obama.

wow none of that made sense. Stupid spell check.

Nov 30, 2010 11:14 AM

Send

DAMN YOU, AUTOCORRECT!

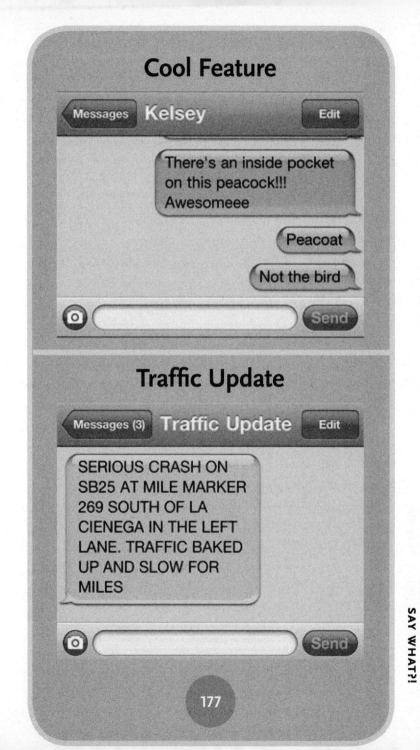

Cool Feature

Kelsey Edit

> There's an inside pocket on this peacock!!! Awesomeee

> Peacoat

> Not the bird

Send

Traffic Update

Messages (3) Traffic Update Edit

> SERIOUS CRASH ON SB25 AT MILE MARKER 269 SOUTH OF LA CIENEGA IN THE LEFT LANE. TRAFFIC BAKED UP AND SLOW FOR MILES

Send

SAY WHAT?!

Random Russian Head Coverings

Looks like it will cost at least $3500. Just estimating, 4 tickets, rental car, 1 week of hotel room, food. Not to mention Olivia will be on solids then, well have to buy jars or babushka

Baby food

Yes babushka. Lol

Phone has been acting really weird lately, it doesn't suggest very good words

Nice.

Send

179

SAY WHAT?!

"Is That Really a Word?!"

A Family of Influence During the Bengal Renaissance (DUH!)

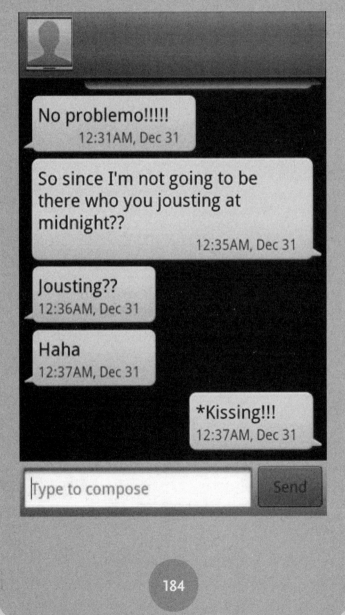

Sisterly Bonding

Stephen Hawking, Is That You?

6

**Textin'
9 to 5:**

Autocorrected
on the Clock

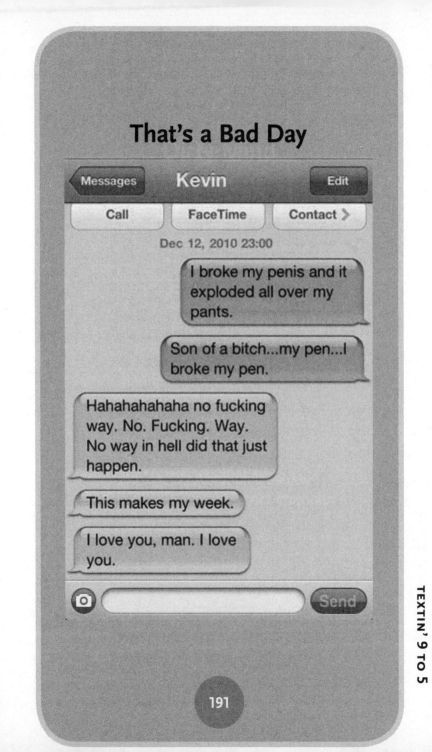

That's a Bad Day

TEXTIN' 9 TO 5

Anger Management

Dec 28, 2010 8:52 PM

So how did the retreat go? I was so bored when I went last year.

Yeah it was pretty dull. Thank God Dave was there. He is hilarious.

I know! So funny. So you guys boned over the weekend eh?

Uh I'm not into dudes. That and my girlfriend would be pissed.

I meant bonded! Sorry, my bad. Autocorrect!

TEXTIN' 9 TO 5

Getting (a)Head in the Workplace

Call | Contact Info

Load Earlier Messages

Dec 11, 2010 6:42 PM

So I have blown my boss twice, and it's not as bad as I thought

WTF

What???

Look at your last text

Lmfao!!!!!!!!! Nose*

DAMN YOU, AUTOCORRECT!

196

Tough Commute

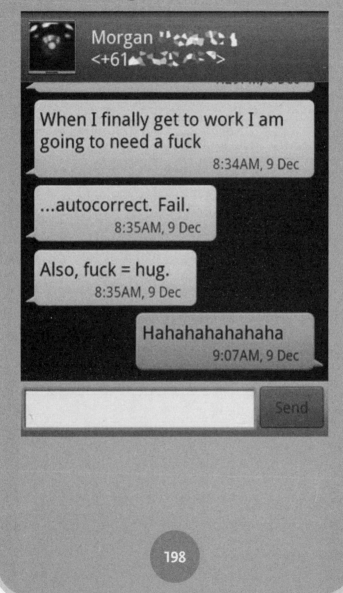

Before the Meeting

Call   Contact Info

Hey Ken, please don't forget to come on me before the meeting. Thanks!

*come get me. That got autocorrected. I sincerely apologize.

Send

DAMN YOU, AUTOCORRECT!

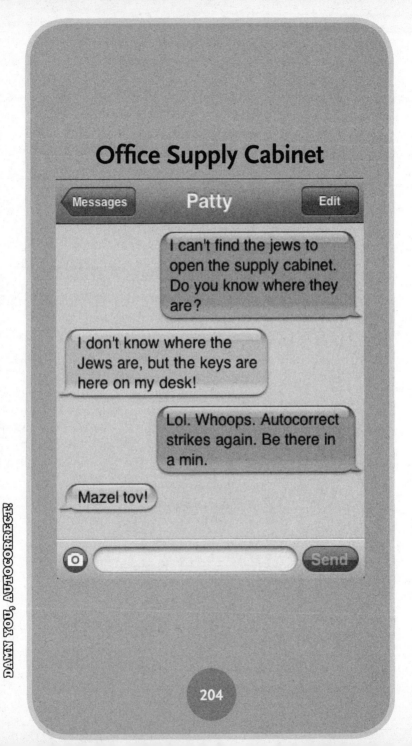

New Position

Messages **Shelface** Edit

yesterday. Hes led me to believe that worst case scenario I'll scramble into abortion here

Wow, autocorrect. Fucking wow. I'll scramble into a preliminary spot here.

Haha

How did it get abortion from preliminary?

No clue

DAMN YOU, AUTOCORRECT!

Extra Hours

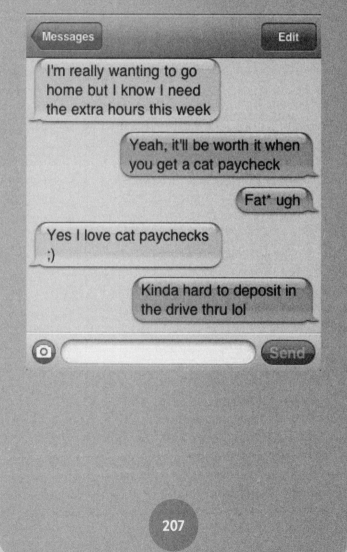

Lost Promotion

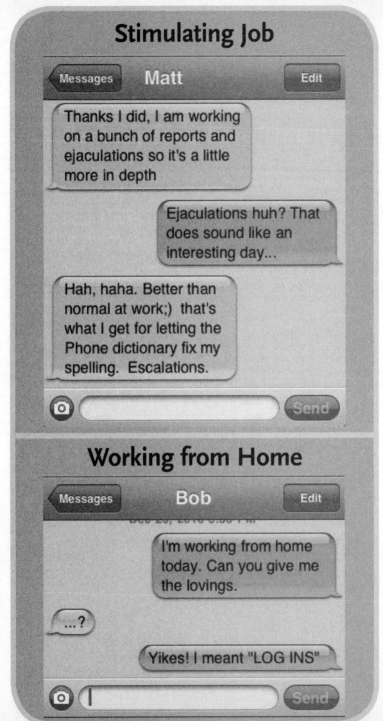

Hooking Up the New Monitor

12/05 19:02

Should i hook up my new monitor through Vga or hdmi?

12/05 19:05

Hdmi. Better penis that way.

wtf. That was supposed to say picture...

Send

DAMN YOU, AUTOCORRECT!

Sounds Dangerous

Messages | **Melis** | **Edit**

Waiting waiting waiting

In Congo by myself

OMG. CONFERENCE room.

And I was just offered some fruitcake!

You really should not be in Congo by yourself. Sounds dangerous. But at least you won't go hungry.

Send

213

Slow Day

DAMN YOU, AUTOCORRECT!

Early Morning Issues

TEXTIN' 9 TO 5

Servers Down

Hey Marcus, our servers have been down since 10. Are you coming in this afternoon at all?

Hi Liz, I can't make it there til at least 4. I'm stuck in this semen til then.

I meant seminar! Well that was awkward!

Ha. Totally. Okay I will let John know.

Send

7

**With Friends
Like These:**

When Friends Let Friends
Get Autocorrected

Creepy Birthday Present

Messages | Edit

Call | Contact Info

What does Megan want for her birthday?

get her the skin graft set

She is Hannibal lecter now? WTF

lol I meant the "skin care" set we talked about from Macy's

Put the lotion in the basket!!!

Send

223

WITH FRIENDS LIKE THESE

Christmas Gifts

Merry Christmas to you too!

What did you get for Christmas?

Dec 26, 2010 01:33 AM

An iPod and cock books.

OMG! You got what for christmas.?

LOL! I mean COOK books. Well, that would be an odd Christmas gift.

O⁺   Send

Fitness Regime

WITH FRIENDS LIKE THESE

Somebody Stage an Intervention

Messages **Wendy** Edit

We're just browsing. We were looking for a crackpot for my mom.

Lol. Crackpot eh? Lmao

Didn't know kohls sold crackpots or that your mom did crack. Lmao

Lol I meant crockpot!

I know tehe

Send

231

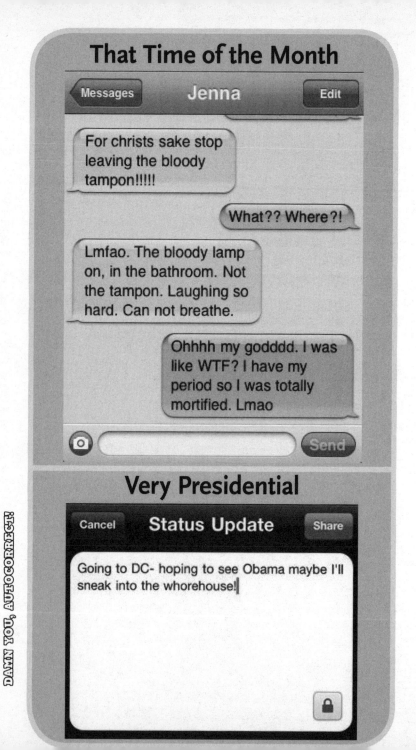

They Make Toilets for That, You Know

Messages **Addi** Edit

What are you up to?

Just shitting on my bed...it feels great.

Ditying*

fining

DEFYING

SITTING DAMMIT*

Okay... Damn just asking....

that's gross btw..hahahaha

Send

Trendy New Paint Color

WITH FRIENDS LIKE THESE

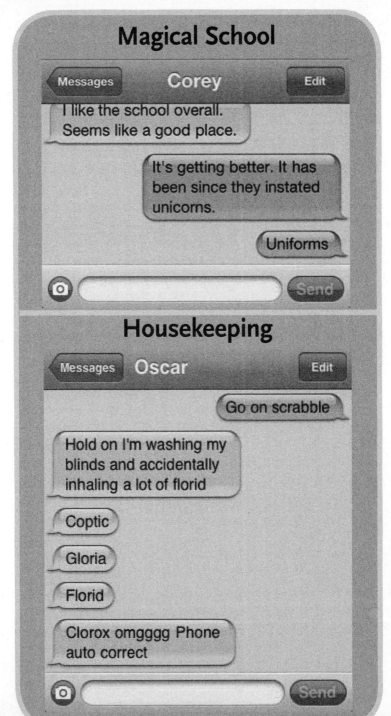

WITH FRIENDS LIKE THESE

Uh, Get Well Soon?

Messages · **Elisabeth** · Edit

Hey girl we can't make it this morning. I've got a anus infection and had to teach with it last night so I'm gonna chill with David and the boys this morning.

Hahaha!!!! Sinus infection! Haha

Gotta love auto correct!!!

Lol, we are all laughing at your post. Feel better:)

Thanks :)

Send

243

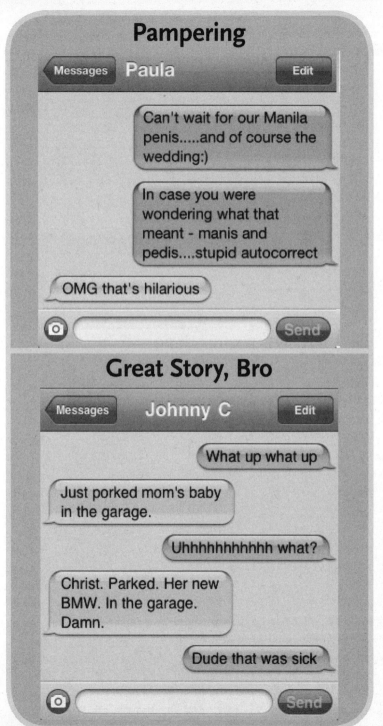

The Wizard of Autocorrect

WITH FRIENDS LIKE THESE

Never Show Up Empty-Handed

02/02: me to tell you that its not a formal thing at all

Alright alright.. What can I bring? I hate showing up someplace without some thank you thong

........thing!!!

Would she like a thong maybe?

Yea definitely don't bring a thank you thong, she might get the wrong impression :) umm I dunno, maybe a desert or something...

Adopting a Dog

WITH FRIENDS LIKE THESE

Dropping Hints

Becki found a watch for Dave. She is excited about it. Glad that is done with.

Very good. Becks is done.

If you are still looking for a suggestion, I would like to have a man-scarf to match my black cock.

My black COAT**, I meant coat. Damn auto correct.

I'm telling mom what you said.

Dad's Christmas Present

WITH FRIENDS LIKE THESE

Bah, Humbug!

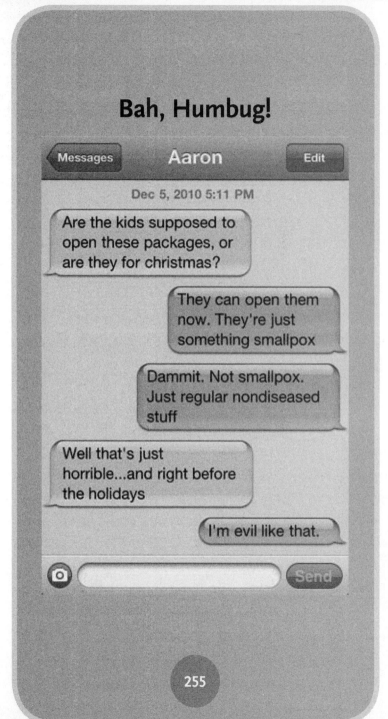

WITH FRIENDS LIKE THESE

Sounds Like a Great Party

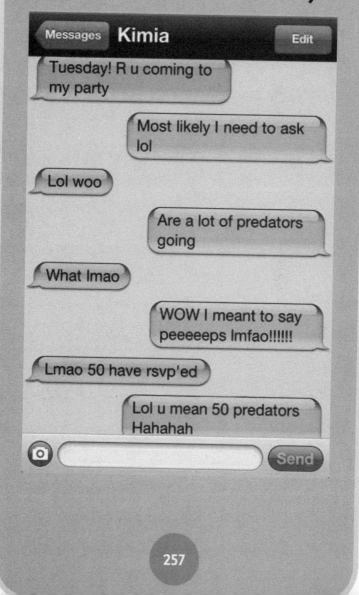

Messages **Kimia** Edit

Tuesday! R u coming to my party

Most likely I need to ask lol

Lol woo

Are a lot of predators going

What lmao

WOW I meant to say peeeeeps lmfao!!!!!!

Lmao 50 have rsvp'ed

Lol u mean 50 predators Hahahah

Send

WITH FRIENDS LIKE THESE

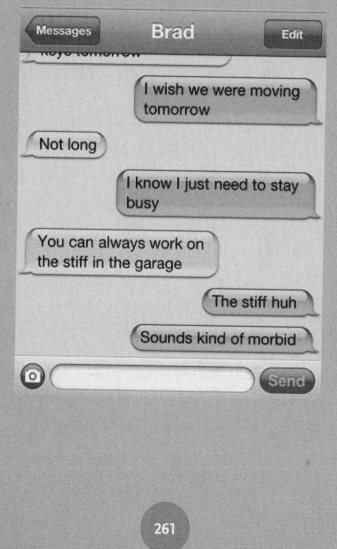

Moving Day

WITH FRIENDS LIKE THESE

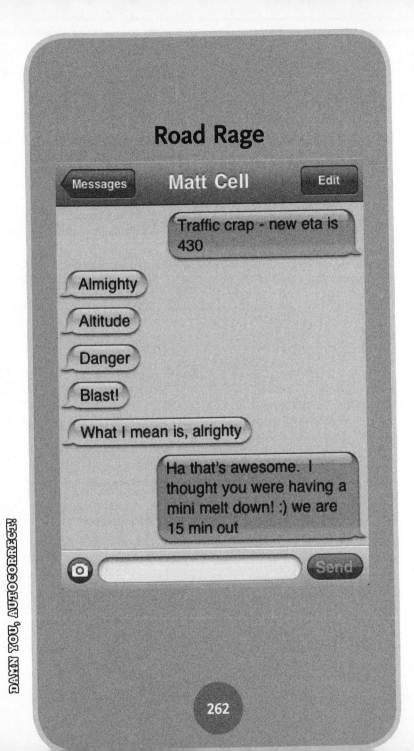

Memorable Pics of Dad

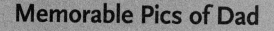

Messages   Edit

> I think my sister took pics of your dads boob at the convention, should I send some to you for the facebook page?

> Booth not boob!! Stupid Phone autocorrect

Hhahahahah!!! I died for a second

> Lol oh man it always does this to me. What a pervert phone

Dont know if its right to put photos of boobs on the site

Send

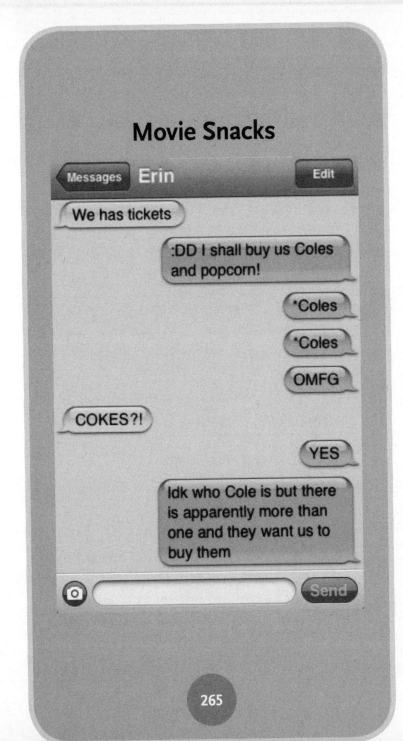

WITH FRIENDS LIKE THESE

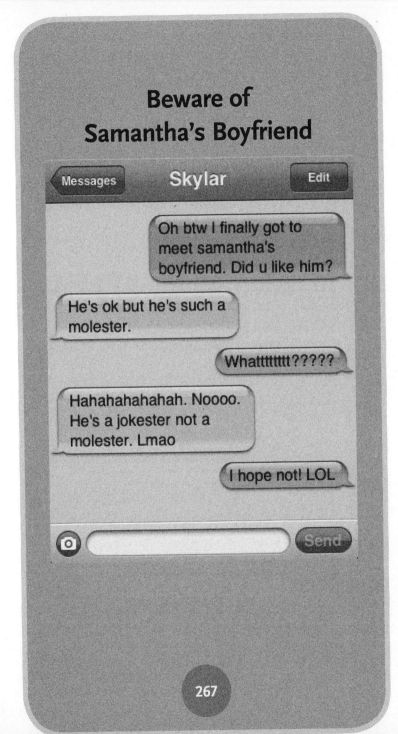

WITH FRIENDS LIKE THESE

Whoops

How's she feeling?

Still very sick. HIV been keeping her in bed all day.

OMG she has HIV?

Oh crap NO. I meant to type "I've been keeping her I'm bed all day" damn auto correct. Sorry for scaring you.

Hahahahaha ya let's not make that mistake again. I just had a heart attack lol

Send

269

Higher Learning

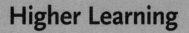

I'll meet you @ 6:00? I'm taking a new fart class. Be done by 5:45.

What type of things do you do in these "FART" classes? Not sure I want to meet up after youve been there for hours! LMAO.

Oh. My. God. ART CLASS. Renaissance Fine Art. No flatulence. I hope. See you at 6?

WITH FRIENDS LIKE THESE

How Festive

WITH FRIENDS LIKE THESE

Bikes from Santa

WITH FRIENDS LIKE THESE

Afterword

TURNING OFF AUTOCORRECT
(NOT THAT YOU'D WANT TO!)

So what if you want to avoid the unfortunate fates of the texters in the book? Is there a way to turn Autocorrect off?

Yes, there is! It's an optional feature that you can elect to shut off at any time.

If you have an iPhone or iPod Touch, tap the Settings icon, then navigate to the General > Keyboard menu. If you have a Droid, go to Menu > Settings > Language & Keyboard > Device Keyboard, and uncheck Auto-replace. If all else fails, refer to the documentation that came with your device for exact directions. That said, why would you want to miss out on all the accidental hilarity! Leave it on! Just remember to proofread before you send something really bad . . . because we'll be watching!

And if you have any great texting fails, feel free to send them my way!

Find DYAC on the web: http://damnyouautocorrect.com

Submission terms and conditions: http://damnyouautocorrect.com/submission-terms-and-conditions/

Twitter: http://twitter.com/damnyouac

E-mail: submit@damnyouautocorrect.com